# Sending a Letter

ROWLAND HILL 1795-1879

Alex Stewart

# W
## FRANKLIN WATTS
### NEW YORK • LONDON • SYDNEY

First published in 1999 by
Franklin Watts
96 Leonard Street
London
EC2A 4XD

Franklin Watts Australia
14 Mars Road
Lane Cove
NSW 2066
Australia

© Franklin Watts 1999

ISBN: 0 7496 3386 7 (hbk)
        0 7496 3584 3 (pbk)
Dewey Decimal Classification 383
A CIP catalogue record for this book is available
from the British Library

Printed in Malaysia

Planning and production by Discovery Books Limited
Editors: Paul Humphrey, Claire Berridge
Design: Ian Winton
Art Director: Robert Walster

Illustrators: Ross Watton, Stefan Chabluk, Terry
Hadler, Joanna Williams

Photographs:
4 Peter Newark's Western Americana, 5 Matthew
McKee/Eye Ubiquitous, 6 E.T. archive, 8 Mary Evans
Picture Library, 10 Peter Newark's Historical Pictures,
11 Mary Evans Picture Library, 12 Peter Newark's
American Pictures, 13 top and bottom Mary Evans
Picture Library, 15 Peter Newark's Western
Americana, 16 Mary Evans Picture Library, 17 top
Mary Evans Picture Library, 17 bottom Peter
Newark's Western Americana, 18 Peter Newark's
Pictures, 20 top Peter Newark's American Pictures, 20
bottom Mary Evans Picture Library, 21 Peter
Newark's Historical Pictures, 22 Mary Evans Picture
Library, 24 E.T. archive, 25 Mary Evans Picture
Library, 28 Peter Hendrie/Image Bank.

Acknowledgement
Discovery Books would like to thank Federal Express
for the loan of material.

# Contents

# Sending messages

Most of us enjoy getting letters in the post. It is fun writing back to our family and friends, too. Many children have pen friends in other countries. Every day, all over the world, postmen and women deliver millions of letters.

A postwoman delivers letters in Sydney, Australia.

## Before writing

There was a time when people didn't write any letters at all. There weren't any pens, paper, stamps or envelopes, either. In fact, there wasn't even any writing.

Before writing was invented, people still sent messages. They blew loud musical instruments, like horns. Their sound was used to warn of danger.

## Smoke signals

Some Native American people used smoke signals to send simple messages. Other native peoples beat out messages on drums.

## Messengers

Before writing was invented, the best way to send long messages was by messenger. A messenger had to be a fast runner with a good memory. His work could be dangerous. Messengers who brought bad news sometimes had their heads cut off!

# The first postal services

Rulers in ancient times used messengers to carry letters around their kingdoms. The first letters were delivered one at a time. The Ancient Egyptians started the first post service 4,000 years ago. It used a network of messengers to carry official post.

In ancient times few people knew how to write. Even kings and queens needed 'scribes' to write letters for them. This Sumerian scribe is writing on clay tablets with a reed pen.

A Sumerian scribe.

## Something to write on

The Ancient Egyptians invented the first kind of paper. It was made from water reeds and was called 'papyrus'. Early writers also wrote on 'parchment', made from dried animal skins. Tsai Lun, a Chinese man, invented the first proper paper about 2,000 years ago. Paper is made by 'pulping' (crushing up) rags or wood. The secret of paper-making took hundreds of years to spread round the world.

## Relay riders

Three thousand years ago, the Chinese invented the relay system. Riders carried the post for an hour or two, then stopped to change the horse or the rider.

## Roman post

The Romans set up the quick and reliable *cursus publicus* or 'public post'. Messengers carried letters along the fine network of Roman roads. All Roman citizens could use the *cursus publicus* – rulers, scholars, traders, priests and even ordinary soldiers.

# Signed and sealed

The first letters were written with brushes. Early pens were made from reeds or large feathers, known as quills.

People used to make their own ink. It was made from all sorts of things, including soot and a dark juice taken from oak trees. Ink was stored in jars or in animal horns.

Writing with a quill and ink in the early seventeenth century.

## Making a quill pen

Make sure an adult helps you with this project! You will need a goose feather, a sharp knife, paper and ink.

1 Cut off the tip of the quill. Check that the inside is clean and hollow.

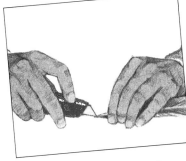

2 Make a vertical slit in the nib (end) of your quill.

3 Dip your pen in the ink, and get writing!

## Seals

As many people did not write their own letters, they needed a way to show that their letters were real. To do this, they put their own 'seal' (an image in wax) on their letters.

## Making a seal

The letter was written, and folded over two or three times. Hot, soft wax was dropped onto the letter to seal it. Then the image was pressed into the wax. When the wax cooled, it turned hard. The image was now fixed into the wax.

Wax seals kept a letter secret. This was very useful before envelopes were invented in the eighteenth century. If you received a letter with a broken seal, then you knew someone had opened it before you!

# Medieval mail

During the Middle Ages rulers, priests, the army and the universities set up and ran their own postal services across Europe. There was a public service in northern Germany. Mounted postmen blew a blast on their horn as they rode through the villages. Anyone with letters to send would bring them out.

▶ A postman delivering letters on foot in the Middle Ages.

▼ This seventeenth-century German postman blows a horn to announce his arrival.

## Postboys

In Britain, innkeepers had to stable horses for use by the king's messengers. These messengers were called postboys. This service was only for the use of the king and government officials, but people across the country also kept horses for hire by messengers carrying letters for rich merchants and nobles.

These fifteenth-century merchants have brought letters from abroad.

## Expensive postal services

Early post services were very expensive. The cost of delivering a letter depended on how far it was going and how heavy it was. The fee was paid by the person receiving the letter, not the one sending it. Only rich people sent and received letters.

# Reliable mail

The first truly national service was set up in 1464 by King Louis XI of France. During the sixteenth and seventeenth centuries postal services across western Europe became much more reliable.

## NEWS! NEWS!!

AARON OLIVER, *Poſt-Rider,* WISHES to inform the Public, that he has extended his Route; and that he now rides thro' the towns of Troy, Piliſtown, Hooſick, Mapletown, part of Bennington and Shaftſbury, Petersburgh, Stephentown, Greenbuſh and Schodack. All commands in his line will be received with thanks, and executed with punctuality. He returns his ſincere thanks to his former cuſtomers; and intends, by unabated diligence, to merit a continuance of their favours.

O'er ruggid hills, aud vallies wide,
He never yet has fail'd to trudge it:
As ſteady as the flowing tide,
He bands about the NORTHERN BUDGET.

June 18, 1799.

## The New World

At the same time, people were beginning to look to the New World for a fresh start in life. In early colonial America people depended on friends, merchants and Native Americans to carry mail for them around the colonies. The first regular mounted mail service in America began in January 1673 between New York and Boston.

An early American post-rider tells people about his service (1799).

## Receiving stations

People wanting to send a letter deposited it at special shops, coffee houses or inns that acted as receiving stations. Mail was then carried to other receiving stations for collection. It was not delivered to people's homes unless they paid an extra fee to a letter carrier.

A London postman with his bell (1820).

▲ A coffee house was the best place to send and receive mail in the 1700s.

## Bellmen

In some cities strolling bellmen walked through the streets. When people heard the bell ringing they would bring out their letters. This saved them a visit to the receiving house.

13

# Mail and stage coaches

Early mail was carried on foot or by mounted postboys. But carrying mail alone could be dangerous. By the eighteenth century many post services carried the mail in horse-drawn coaches. The coaches carried passengers as well as mail. They travelled along special post roads that were better than the normal roads.

## The stage

Mail coaches made their journeys in stages, so they were also known as stage coaches. At the end of each stage, they stopped at a coaching inn or a relay station. Here they changed horses and picked up or put down passengers and mail. Long distance mail therefore took a long time to get to its destination.

# The Pony Express

To speed up mail deliveries in the USA, the Pony Express mail service was set up in 1860. Mail was carried in saddle bags by brave young riders across the wild west of America. There were 80 riders, 430 horses and 190 post stations. The riders had to change horses in only two minutes. The journey time for the 3,200-km (2,000-mile) route was 11 days.

Sacramento, California

St. Joseph, Missouri

Route of the Pony Express

## Highwaymen

Mail coaches carried an armed guard to look after the passengers and mail. He was needed in case the coach was attacked by robbers or highwaymen.

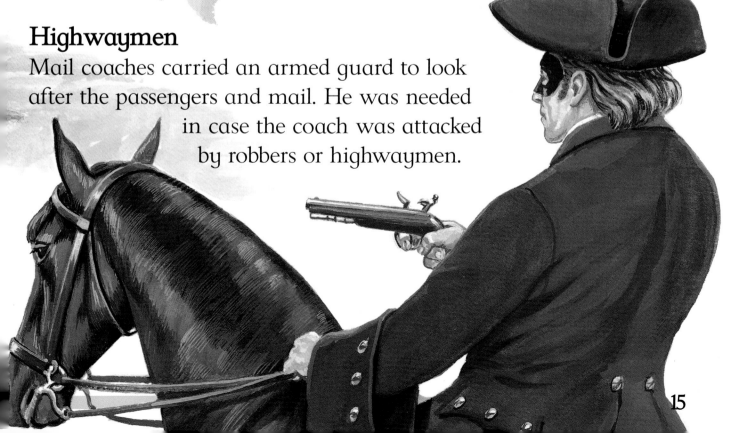

# Post offices

By the beginning of the nineteenth century proper post offices were replacing the inns, shops and coffee houses as receivers and collectors of mail. But there were still few post boxes.

London's busy general post office in 1849.

If you wanted to post a letter you had to take it to the nearest post office. There it would be weighed and a charge would be made depending upon how heavy it was and how far it was travelling. It became more common for the sender to pay the postage. Letters were stamped to show that postage had been paid.

## Special delivery

Letters would be delivered to the post offices of big cities and people could either collect them for themselves or pay a little extra for the mail to be delivered to their door by carriers.

## Country post

People living in country areas still had to collect their mail from the town post offices. This was difficult for these people, especially for those that lived in remote areas, where it could take many days to reach the nearest post office.

Sending letters was still very expensive and most ordinary people could not afford to do it.

A nineteenth-century American postman runs to catch the post as the stage coach thunders past.

# Stamps

In 1837 a man called Rowland Hill introduced a new way of sending the mail around Britain. He suggested that the post office should have a standard list of charges based on weight only, not distance, and that postage should only be paid by the sender. He also suggested that a label should be stuck on letters to show that prepayment had been made. The modern postage stamp was born!

Sir Rowland Hill.

## Penny post

In 1840 the British post office began charging one penny to deliver a normal letter anywhere in the country. The person sending the letter paid, and stuck a one-penny stamp onto an envelope. People no longer had to pay letter carriers to deliver mail to their doors, wherever they lived. The idea was a great success.

# Designing a stamp

You will need paper, coloured pencils or paints, scissors and paste.

1 Draw the shape
of your stamp on
a piece of paper
and colour it in.

2 Write the value
on your stamp and
the country it has
come from.

3 Cut out your stamp and
stick it onto an envelope.
But don't try to send a letter
with your stamp on it!

## Post boxes

Other countries began using stamps. At last, everyone
could afford to use the mail, and there was a huge
increase in the number of letters. More and more post
boxes sprang up in towns and country areas.

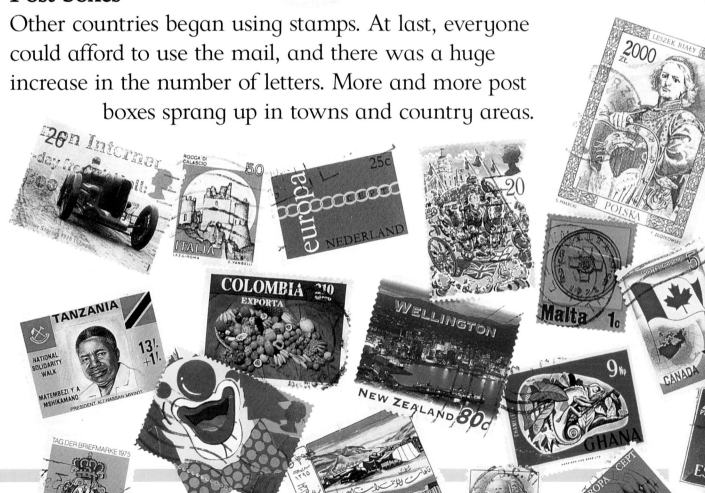

From the middle of the nineteenth century onwards, several inventions greatly speeded up the delivery of the post. The first was the railway. Mail trains carried sacks of letters hundreds of kilometres in only a few hours. Mail wagons picked up mail without even stopping! Later, motor vans made delivery even quicker.

Almost a hundred years separate the mail train advertised above and this 1930s' van.

## Sorting offices

As more people learned to read and write, they sent more letters. By 1900, millions of letters were delivered each day. More post offices were needed. More post boxes were set up in towns and villages. Huge sorting offices were built to sort out the mail and send it to the right address. Machines were invented to print postmarks and sort mail automatically.

▲ An American post box from the early 1900s.

◀ A British post box from the 1800s.

## Letter boxes

In the past, when very few letters were sent, a letter was addressed with just a name and a town or district. Now that everyone was receiving letters, each house needed a name or number and a letter box.

▼ Can you tell which of these letters is old and which is new?

Doctor B. Harrington
Beverley
East Riding of Yorkshire

Carla Rainer
Flat 5
17 Shatton Road
Eddington
Greater Manchester
M26 6AD

 # Overseas mail

The first official international sea mail services started in the seventeenth century, linking the ports of Europe with their colonies overseas. Mail was also carried privately by ships' captains. The mail was collected in inns and coffee houses in the ports where ships arrived and departed.

The mail for India is loaded onto this ship in the French port of Boulogne in 1844.

In 1639 Richard Fairbanks' tavern in Boston became the official place for collection and receipt of mail arriving in Massachusetts from England. Other American states soon followed and set up official receiving stations for international mail.

## Mail steamers

Sea mail was carried in sailing ships. The service was not very reliable because it depended on the wind. The first steam ships were built in the nineteenth century. Mail steamers were quicker and more reliable than sailing ships.

**Special Par Delivery exprès**

**G-AAGX**
HANNIBAL
IMPERIAL AIRWAYS LONDON

AIR MAIL

**AIR MAIL** PAR AVION

By air mail *Par avion*

By air mail *Par avion*

## Air mail

When aircraft were invented in the twentieth century, long-distance mail services became even faster. Air mail was first tried in 1911 and by the 1920s it was firmly established. By the 1990s a letter could be sent from America to Europe in just 24 hours.

Lawrence and Elmer Sperry Aviation Pioneers
US Airmail 39

# Down the wire

In the nineteenth century scientists invented a completely new way of sending messages. This was the telegraph. The words of a message were turned into electric signals and sent down a wire. At the other end of the wire, the signals were changed back into words.

An early machine for sending and receiving telegrams.

## Morse code

In 1843 Samuel Morse invented his famous Morse code for changing words into electric signals.

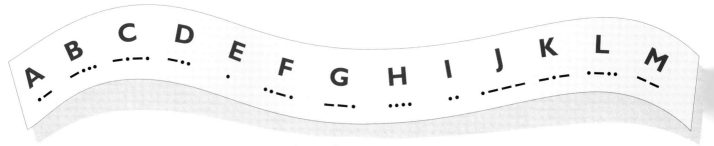

The code used short signals (dots) and long signals (dashes). An 'A', for example, was a dot followed by a dash. A telegraph operator needed lots of practice to quickly turn a stream of dots and dashes into words. Later, a teleprinter did the job automatically.

## Telegraph offices

Telegraph messages were sent to post offices or telegraph offices. The office receiving the message typed it out as a short letter, or telegram. This was delivered as quickly as possible. Since telegrams were expensive, they were used mainly for short and important messages, such as wedding congratulations or birth announcements.

International
**TELEGRAM**

Peter Bendick
45 Dean Street
Farmdown
Doncaster
D12 3DG

MANCHESTER
6.V.97
M3

A telegraph office.

# Today's post

The post code is a modern invention. When we address an envelope, we finish with this code. Then our letter is ready for posting (1).

After mail has been collected from a post box (2), it is taken to a sorting office.

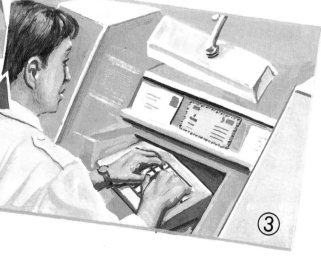

Letters used to be sorted by hand. Nowadays, a machine puts electronic marks on the letters, according to their post codes, to say where they are going (3).

## Special delivery

Couriers deliver thousands of letters, packets and parcels every day. In order to deliver their post as quickly as possible, couriers take it by motorbike, van and plane. They can carry a letter or parcel half way around the world and deliver it the very next morning.

26

## Electronic sorting

The letters move along a belt into a sorting machine that reads the marks. The machine steers all letters with similar marks into the same bag (4).

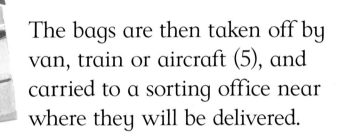

The bags are then taken off by van, train or aircraft (5), and carried to a sorting office near where they will be delivered.

## Delivering today's mail

Here the letters are sorted again into districts, streets and houses. Postmen and women collect the letters for their own rounds, and set off to deliver them. The journey finally ends when a letter comes through your letter box, or is put in your mail box outside (6).

In the 1980s it became quite common to send letters by fax. Once a letter was written, it was fed into a fax machine. This scanned the letter and sent it to its address electronically. A fax machine at the other end printed it out, with no need for postmen, sorting offices or even stamps.

2 Message sent to local server.

How an e-mail message is sent.

②

1 Message typed in by person on computer.

## E-mail

By the 1990s there was yet another way of sending a letter. This was by e-mail. The letter was written straight onto a computer screen. It was then sent via the Internet direct to another computer and read on-screen. An e-mail letter travelled to the other side of the world in seconds. And no one had even used a pen and paper!

28

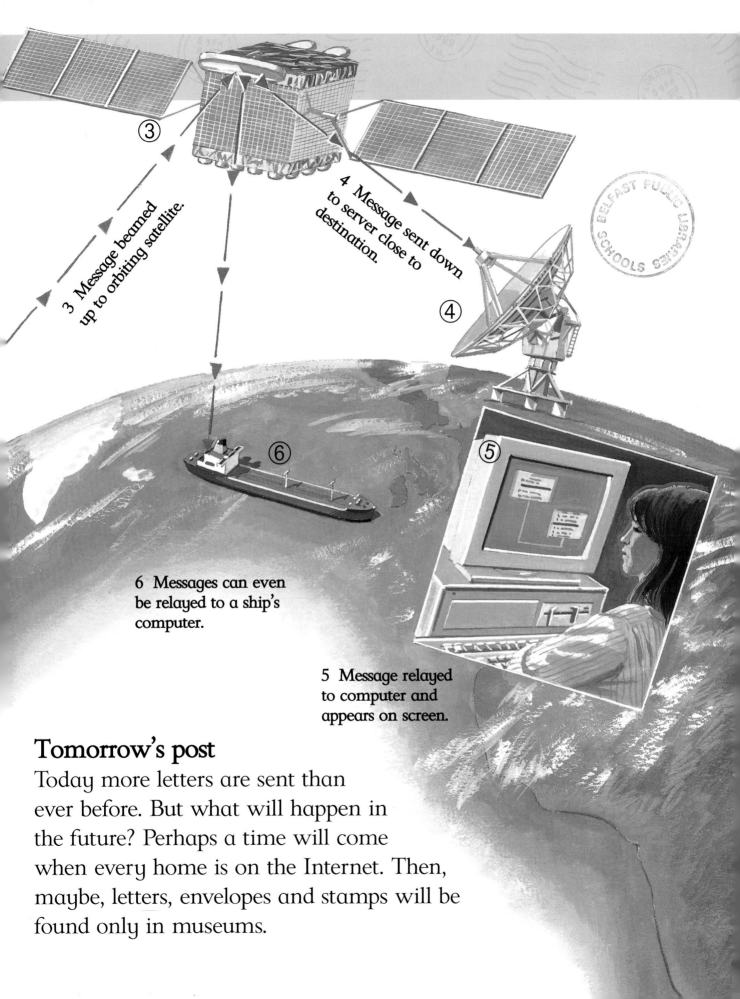

③

3 Message beamed up to orbiting satellite.

4 Message sent down to server close to destination.

④

⑤

⑥

6 Messages can even be relayed to a ship's computer.

5 Message relayed to computer and appears on screen.

## Tomorrow's post

Today more letters are sent than ever before. But what will happen in the future? Perhaps a time will come when every home is on the Internet. Then, maybe, letters, envelopes and stamps will be found only in museums.

# Timeline

## BC

| c 3,500 | Writing invented in Sumeria. |
| c 2,000 | Postal system begins in Egypt. |
| c 1,000 | Postal system begins in China. |
| c 300 | Egyptians using reed pens. |

## AD

| c 105 | Tsai Lun makes the first paper. |
| c 1500 | Pencils being used. |
| 1500s | Postal service running between Brussels, Vienna and Madrid. |
| 1721 | Regular postal service between London and America begins. |
| 1828 | John Mitchell introduces machine-made steel pens. |
| 1838 | Mail first sorted on board a moving mail train. |
| 1839 | Electric telegraph invented. |
| 1840 | Penny post system begins. |
| 1843 | Morse code invented. |
| 1860 | Pony Express mail service set up in western USA. |
| 1867 | Christopher Scholes makes first reliable typewriter. |
| 1884 | LE Waterman makes the first reliable fountain pen. |
| 1911 | Air mail first tried. |
| 1919 | First air mail service begins between London and Paris. |
| 1938 | Ladislao Biro produces the first reliable ballpoint pen. |
| 1946 | First electronic computer built. |
| 1960s | Pens with fibre tips introduced. |
| 1969 | Internet set up. |
| 1980s | Fax machines available for home use. |
| 1990s | E-mail available for home use. |

# Glossary

**Courier**  A special delivery service that takes post all around the world as quickly as possible.

**Papyrus**  A kind of paper made from reeds.

**Parchment**  Dried animal skin used for writing on.

**Quill**  A long feather used as a dip pen.

**Relay**  Delivering mail by passing it from one carrier to another.

**Scribe**  Someone who does other people's writing for them.

**Seal**  The wax image that a sender puts on a letter to prove that they have written it.

**Sorting office**  An office where letters are sorted for delivery.

**Stage coach**  A coach that is pulled by different teams of horses during its journey.

**Telegram**  A written message that is sent by telegraph.

**Telegraph**  A way of sending a message down a wire by electricity.

**Teleprinter**  A machine that prints out a message sent by telegraph.

# Further reading

**Brimner, Larry Dane,** *E Mail*, True Books, 1998

**Burns, Peggy,** *The Post*, Wayland, 1994

**Farrell, Sue,** *To The Post Office With Mama*, New York, 1994

**Fyson, Nance,** *History of Britain's Post*, Young Library, 1992

**Landstrom, Olof,** *Will Goes To The Post Office*, R & S Books, 1994

**Thomson, Ruth,** *In The Post*, Black, 1990

**Ramsay, Helena,** *Where Does A Letter Go?* Evans, 1996

# Index